Energy

Andrew Solway

Chicago, Illinois

www.heinemannraintree.com
Visit our website to find out
more information about
Heinemann-Raintree books.

To order:
☎ Phone 888-454-2279
💻 Visit www.heinemannraintree.com
to browse our catalog and order online.

© 2011 Raintree
an imprint of Capstone Global Library, LLC
Chicago, Illinois

Edited by Andrew Farrow, Adam Miller, and
 Diyan Leake
Designed by Philippa Jenkins
Original illustrations © Capstone Global Library
 Limited 2011
Illustrated by Capstone Global Library, Gordon Hurden,
 and Kerry Flaherty
Picture research by Hannah Taylor
Originated by Capstone Global Library Limited
Printed in the United States of America by
 Worzalla Publishing

14 13 12 11 10
10 9 8 7 6 5 4 3 2 1

Library of Congress Cataloging-in-Publication Data
Solway, Andrew.
 The scientists behind energy / Andrew Solway.
  p. cm.—(Sci-hi. Scientists)
 Includes bibliographical references and index.
 ISBN 978-1-4109-4045-2 (hc)—ISBN 978-1-4109-
4052-0 (pb) 1. Scientists—Juvenile literature. 2. Power
resources—History—Juvenile literature. 3. Force and
energy—Juvenile literature. I. Title.
 Q141.S5643 2011
 621.042'2—dc22   2010031258

Acknowledgments
The author and publishers are grateful to the following
for permission to reproduce copyright material:
Alamy Images pp. **4** (© The Art Gallery Collection), **11**
(© Interfoto), **13** bottom (© The Art Gallery Collection),
22 bottom (© Dennis MacDonald), **23** (© Mary Evans
Picture Library), **28–29** (© Geoff Kirby), **31** (© World
History Archive), **37** (© Paul Glendell); Corbis pp. **7** (The
Gallery Collection), **9** top (Danielle Sosa), **15** (Transtock/
Robert Genat), **17** (epa/Matthias Hiekel), **32** (Igor
Kostin), **33** (epa); ETH Zurich p. **39**; Getty Images pp. **9**
bottom (FS top/Martin Diebel), **13** top (SSPL), **18** (Time
Life Pictures), **19** (Ross Setford), **26** (Hulton Archive),
35 (Time Life Pictures/Alfred Eisenstaedt); istockphoto
p. **12** (© Maxim Petrichuk); Julie Fraser p. **41**; Courtesy
MIT Museum p. **34**; NASA p. **40**; Gustav Nyström,
Uppsala University p. **21** top and bottom; Pelamis Wave
Power **contents page** bottom, p. **38**; Science Photo
Library pp. **16** top and bottom (Library of Congress/
George Grantham Bain Collection), **36** (David Nunuk);
shutterstock background images and design elements
throughout, **contents page** top (© Ivan Montero
Martinez), pp. **5** (© Arteki), **8** (Wth), **22** top (© Ivan
Montero Martinez); Still Pictures p. **27** (Markus Scholz/
argus); Vanderbilt University p. **25**.

Main cover photograph of a scientist working at
CERN (the European particle physics laboratory) near
Geneva, Switzerland, reproduced with permission of
Science Photo Library (CERN); inset cover photograph
reproduced with permission of istockphoto (© Igor
Goncharenko).

The publisher would like to thank literary consultants
Marla Conn and Nancy Harris and content consultant
Suzy Gazlay for their assistance in the preparation of
this book.

Disclaimer
All the Internet addresses (URLs) given in this book were
valid at the time of going to press. However, due to the
dynamic nature of the Internet, some addresses may
have changed, or sites may have changed or ceased to
exist since publication. While the author and publisher
regret any inconvenience this may cause readers, no
responsibility for any such changes can be accepted by
either the author or the publisher.

Contents

When did electricity become the new source of energy? Find out on page 22!

What is Pelamis? Turn to page 38 to find out!

Some words are shown in bold, **like this**. These words are explained in the glossary. You will find important information and definitions underlined, <u>like this</u>.

WHAT IS Energy?

It has taken us hundreds of years to understand what energy is, and how to use it. The first person to use the word *energy* in a scientific way was a brilliant scientist and thinker named Thomas Young. Since his time, scientists have discovered new forms of energy and have found ways to put energy to use.

THOMAS YOUNG

LIVED: 1773–1829

NATIONALITY: British

FAMOUS FOR: Being the first to use the word *energy* as a scientific term

DID YOU KNOW? Young could speak many languages. He helped to translate the writing on the Rosetta Stone. This is a stone from ancient Egypt that has the same piece of writing on it in three different languages. Translating the Rosetta Stone gave scholars the key to understanding Egyptian hieroglyphics (writing that is made up of pictures rather than words).

GETTING THINGS GOING

Energy is what makes things happen. Energy from the Sun, for example, makes plants grow. Without the plants there would be no food for animals, or humans. Sunlight also powers the movement of the oceans, the wind, and the weather.

The energy we get from food keeps us moving. Humans have also found ways to harness energy for other uses. We use the energy in **petroleum** (oil) and gas to heat homes and offices. Petroleum also powers the engines in cars, ships, and planes. Electricity is another form of energy. It powers everything from trains to cell phones.

In this book you can learn about some of the scientists who have increased our understanding of energy. Find out who proved that Newton got something wrong, and learn whose new discovery broke his equipment. Meet the scientists who are working today to help us produce cleaner energy, and to use less of it.

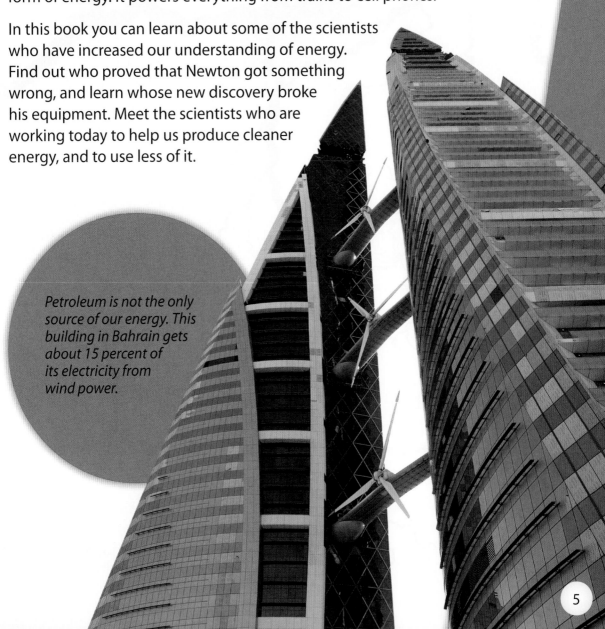

Petroleum is not the only source of our energy. This building in Bahrain gets about 15 percent of its electricity from wind power.

MOVEMENT ENERGY

One of the first types of energy to be studied was **kinetic energy** (movement energy). The British scientist Sir Isaac Newton was one of the first to study movement scientifically. Newton developed three laws of motion. These were a set of rules that could explain all the **forces** (pushes or pulls)involved when objects are moving.

Newton's laws of motion were a great step forward. But when he looked at the energy of movement, Newton got things wrong. The scientist who revealed Newton's mistake was a French mathematician named Émilie du Châtelet.

A BRILLIANT EDUCATION

Émilie's father had an important job at the court of the French king, Louis XIV. She was a very clever and talented child. Her father arranged for her to have the best teaching in math, science, languages, and literature. She also learned how to fence (sword fight), ride, dance, and play the harpsichord.

When she was 19 years old, Émilie married the Marquis (Lord) du Châtelet-Lomont. She had three children, but continued to study and learn.

TRANSLATING NEWTON

In the 1730s, Émilie du Châtelet became interested in Isaac Newton's work. She began a French translation of his most important book, *Mathematical Principles*.

In 1740, du Châtelet published a book of her own, called *Institutions de Physique* (*Lessons in Physics*). In this she explained the ideas of the leading scientists of the time. She looked at the work of Newton, and of Newton's great rival, the German scientist Gottfried Leibniz. She found that, on one topic, Newton had gotten it wrong!

This painting shows Émilie du Châtelet working at her desk. It was difficult in the 1700s for a woman to work and write as a scientist. Du Châtelet and the writer and thinker Voltaire wrote a book together called Elements of Newton's Philosophy. But when the book was published, only Voltaire was listed as the author.

ÉMILIE DU CHÂTELET

LIVED: 1706–1749

NATIONALITY: French

FAMOUS FOR: Showing the correct relationship between the kinetic energy of a moving object and the speed at which it is traveling

DID YOU KNOW? Du Châtelet was a friend of Voltaire, who said that she was "a great man whose only fault was being a woman."

Turn the page to find out what happens next...

NEWTON'S MISTAKE

In her book *Institutions de Physique*, Émilie du Châtelet showed that Newton was wrong about the energy an object has when it is moving. Newton thought that the object's energy changed in line with its speed. He said that an object traveling at 20 kilometers per hour has twice as much energy as when it travels at 10 kilometers per hour. And at 40 kilometers per hour, the object has four times as much energy as at 10 kilometers per hour.

However, du Châtelet showed that, in fact, the kinetic energy (movement energy) of an object changes in line with the **square** of its speed. So, an object traveling at 20 kilometers per hour has *four times* (2 × 2) as much energy as at 10 kilometers per hour; at 40 kilometers per hour it has 16 times (4 × 4) as much energy as at 10 kilometers per hour. Du Châtelet took ideas from Newton's rival Leibniz to prove her point. She supported them with evidence from experiments done by the Dutch scientist Willem Gravesande.

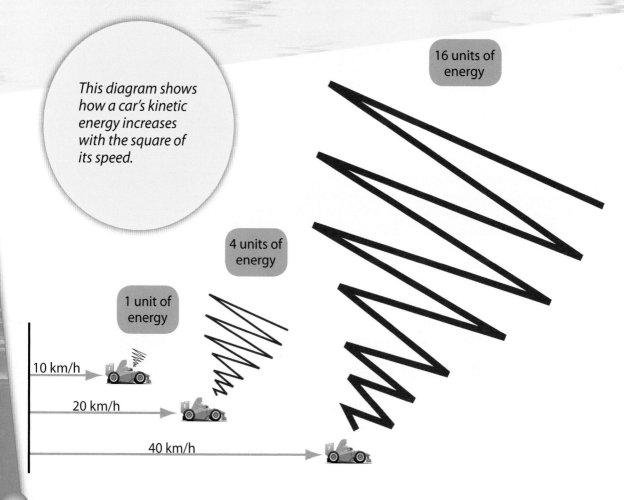

This diagram shows how a car's kinetic energy increases with the square of its speed.

16 units of energy

4 units of energy

1 unit of energy

10 km/h

20 km/h

40 km/h

The kinetic energy of an object depends on its mass (weight) as well as its speed. This aircraft carrier has more kinetic energy than the boats around it, even though the smaller boats are moving faster. This is because it is so much heavier than the boats.

CRASHING CARS FOR SAFETY

A moving car with a driver and passengers has a lot of kinetic energy. Émilie du Châtelet's proof showed that the amount of kinetic energy rises very quickly as a car increases in speed.

In a crash, the kinetic energy is suddenly reduced to zero. This can injure or kill the people inside the car. All cars have safety features to help reduce the effects of a crash. For example, the front of the car is designed to crumple. This absorbs some of the energy of the crash. Seat belts and airbags stop passengers from hitting the dashboard or windshield.

Crash-test dummies make it possible to test safety features such as airbags.

New cars are tested for safety at a crash test center. Each car is tested in several types of crash. The driver and passengers are replaced by crash-test dummies. These contain instruments that measure the forces on the dummies during the crash.

FO4305OZ02

9

Heat Comes into the Mix

You zoom down a hill on your bike, then at the bottom you put on the brakes. A few seconds before you had loads of kinetic energy, now you have none. Where has it all gone?

This question puzzled scientists until the 1800s. Then two men, Julius Robert van Mayer of Germany and James Prescott Joule of England, found an explanation.

LEARNING FROM THE BODY

Von Mayer trained as a doctor in Germany. In 1840 he went on a year-long voyage to the East Indies (now Indonesia). During his trip, von Mayer began studying the body's energy. At the time it was thought that the body burned oxygen for heat. <u>Von Mayer suggested that energy from food provides the **fuel** for body heat and for the work that the muscles do.</u>

When he returned to Germany, von Mayer published his ideas. He suggested that heat and work (movement) are both kinds of energy, and that they can be changed into each other. He also measured how much heat a particular amount of movement would produce. However, his ideas were ignored.

MOVING PARTICLES

It might not be obvious, but heat is a type of kinetic energy. All substances are made of very tiny pieces of matter called particles. Heat energy is the movement of these particles. In a solid, the particles cannot move much, they just vibrate backwards and forwards. In a liquid, the particles can move around and slide past each other. In a gas, the particles rush around at high speed, filling any container they are put into.

JULIUS ROBERT VON MAYER

LIVED: 1814–1878

NATIONALITY: German

FAMOUS FOR: The idea that the body is fueled by energy from food

DID YOU KNOW? Von Mayer was so upset that other scientists ignored his work that he had a breakdown. He spent most of the 1850s in mental hospitals.

WRONG IDEAS!

In 1848 von Mayer worked out that if the Sun was burning, it should run out of energy in only 5,000 years. He suggested that it was fueled by meteorites (rocks from space) crashing into it.

PADDLE WHEELS IN A BARREL

In Manchester, England, meanwhile, a young man named James Joule was working in his father's brewery (beer factory) and studying science in his spare time. Joule first became interested in electricity. He showed that electricity flowing through a wire produced heat in the wire. He also said that heat, electricity, and work were all forms of energy. Joule believed that one form of energy could be converted (changed) into another.

Other scientists ignored Joule's ideas. So he began a series of experiments to show that movement can be converted into heat. In his most famous experiment in 1845, he used a falling weight to turn a paddle wheel in a container of water. As the paddle wheel turned, it heated the water.

CONSERVATION OF ENERGY

Other scientists eventually accepted Joule's and von Mayer's ideas. They had proved that movement, heat, and electricity are all forms of energy. They also proved that one form can be converted into another. Scientists realized that <u>energy is never created or destroyed, it is simply converted from one form into another</u>.

So when we stop a bike after zooming down a hill, where *does* the kinetic energy go? To find the answer, feel the brake pads. The brakes heat up as the bike slows down. The bike's kinetic energy has been converted into heat.

This biker's kinetic energy is transformed into heat when he puts the brakes on.

James Joule used this equipment for one of his experiments. He turned the paddle wheel in a beaker of water. The movement heated the water, and Joule measured the temperature change to find how much heat was produced.

JAMES PRESCOTT JOULE

LIVED: 1818–1889

NATIONALITY: British

FAMOUS FOR: Showing how heat and kinetic energy are connected

DID YOU KNOW? Joule's name has been given to the measurement used to describe a unit of energy—the **joule**.

TURNING HEAT INTO MOVEMENT

Joule and von Mayer showed that kinetic energy could be turned into heat. This is important to know. However, it is not as useful as turning heat into movement. This is what happens in a heat engine. The engines in cars, trucks, ships, and aircraft are all heat engines.

STEAM POWER

The very first heat engines were steam engines. Thomas Newcomen developed the first practical steam engine around 1712. It was used to pump water out of mines. Over the next 100 years, engineers such as James Watt improved Newcomen's engine. By the 1800s, steam engines were powering trains, ships, and the machinery in many factories.

A SPINNING ENGINE

Even the best steam engines were not very **efficient**. They did not convert much of the energy in the fuel into movement. In the 1880s, British engineer Charles Parsons began to work on a much more efficient kind of steam engine. Instead of pushing a part called a piston up and down, the new engine used steam to make a **turbine** (a kind of fan or propeller) spin around.

HOW A HEAT ENGINE WORKS

A heat engine works using a liquid or gas known as a working fluid. The fluid is first heated up by burning some kind of fuel. <u>When a liquid or gas is heated, it expands (gets bigger)</u>. As it expands, the fluid produces a force that can be used to do work.

In many engines, the fluid is inside cylinders with pistons in them. When the fluid expands, it pushes the pistons in turn so that they move up and down.

In a turbine engine, the expanding gas or steam rushes through the turbine blades and makes them spin.

In a jet engine, hot gases are pushed out of the back of the engine in a powerful jet.

The engine of this drag racer has four cylinders on each side.

This photo shows Charles Parsons's boat Turbinia *at full steam.*

GENERATORS AND SHIPS

Steam turbines spin much faster than other kinds of engines. This makes them ideal for turning **generators** (machines that produce electricity—see page 20). By the beginning of the twentieth century, steam turbines were being used in many **power plants** (factory where electricity is produced) .

SIR CHARLES PARSONS

LIVED:	1854–1931
NATIONALITY:	British
FAMOUS FOR:	Developing the first successful steam turbine engine
DID YOU KNOW?	Parsons was the son of an Irish lord. He earned a degree in math from Cambridge University. But when he left the university he went to work as an apprentice (on-the-job trainee) in an engineering firm.

Parsons also designed steam turbines to power ships. In 1895, he built a small turbine-powered ship called *Turbinia*. He wanted to show how well turbines worked in ships. He also hoped to persuade the British navy to use his steam turbines in their ships. In 1897, Parsons "gate crashed" the Naval Review at Spithead in England. The navy's best ships were paraded before Queen Victoria. *Turbinia* weaved in and out between the navy's ships. It traveled so fast that no vessel could catch it. Within a few years of this demonstration, naval ships and ocean liners around the world were being fitted with Parsons turbines.

HERO'S STEAM JET

In around the year 50 CE, nearly 1,700 years before Newcomen built his steam engine, the ancient Greek philosopher Hero of Alexandria made a steam-powered spinning "jet." Hero's engine was a ball that could spin on an axle, with two nozzles sticking out. When the ball was heated, the water inside it boiled, and powerful jets of steam shot out of the nozzles. This made the ball spin around.

In a modern steam turbine, the steam enters the turbine at high pressure.

Electrical Energy

When Parsons developed the steam turbine, large-scale use of electricity was just beginning (see page 22). Engineers began to build power plants that made electricity using large generators. But <u>the first electric power supply was the battery</u>.

PORTABLE POWER

The Italian scientist Alessandro Volta made the first battery in 1800. It was made of disks of two different metals, separated by pads of cardboard soaked in salt solution. The contact between the metals and the salt produced electricity.

Today's batteries are portable sources of energy for everything from watches to Mars rover vehicles. Most are made from metals. In the 1970s, the Japanese scientist Hideki Shirakawa made a discovery that led to a new kind of battery, made entirely from plastic.

As well as making the first battery (left), Volta sent perhaps the first ever long-distance electrical signal. He used a wire 50 kilometers (32 miles) long to send electricity between the Italian towns of Como and Milan, where it made a pistol fire.

A SILVERY FILM

Hideki Shirakawa is a chemist who was interested in making new kinds of plastic. In 1967 he was working on a plastic called polyacetylene. Scientists thought polyacetylene might be able to conduct electricity (allow electricity to flow through it).

In one of Shirakawa's experiments, an accident led to an important discovery. A student made a mistake when preparing the plastic. Instead of coming out as a black powder, the polyacetylene he made was a thin, silvery film.

HIDEKI SHIRAKAWA

BORN: 1936

NATIONALITY: Japanese

FAMOUS FOR: Discovering plastics that conduct electricity

DID YOU KNOW? At school, Shirakawa wrote an essay saying he wanted to be a scientist studying plastics. When he won a **Nobel Prize** in 2000, he was amazed to see his school essay printed in the newspapers. Reporters had dug out a copy from Shirakawa's old school.

CONDUCTING PLASTICS

Shirakawa worked out why the plastic had turned out as a silvery film. The student had put far too much **catalyst** in the mixture. (A catalyst is a substance that makes a change in a substance happen faster.)

Professor Alan MacDiarmid was interested in Shirakawa's discovery. He invited Shirakawa to work for a year in the United States. While he was working in the USA, Shirakawa tried adding a chemical called bromine to the polyacetylene. When he measured how well the new material conducted electricity, the reading was so high it broke the meter. The first conducting plastic had been discovered.

Turn the page to find out more about batteries and generators...

ELECTROMAGNETISM

Batteries are important for portable electricity. But <u>most of the electricity we use today is made using generators</u>. These rely on the connection between electricity and magnetism. The Danish scientist Hans Christian Ørsted showed that when electricity flows through a wire, the wire becomes magnetic. Then British scientist Michael Faraday showed that <u>if a wire is moved near a magnet, electricity flows through the wire</u>.

These two discoveries are at the heart of modern generators. <u>Generators work by spinning a coil of wire within a circle of magnets</u>. Faraday showed that as the coil spins, an electric current flows. In modern generators, the magnets surrounding the coil are **electromagnets**. An electromagnet uses Ørsted's discovery. It produces magnetism by sending an electric current through a coil of wire.

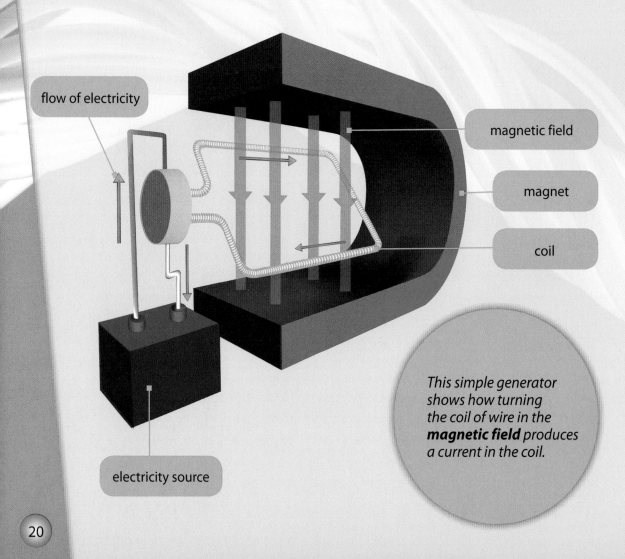

flow of electricity

magnetic field

magnet

coil

electricity source

*This simple generator shows how turning the coil of wire in the **magnetic field** produces a current in the coil.*

PAPER BATTERIES

A team of Swedish scientists led by Professor Maria Strømme has found a way to make a battery on paper (left). The battery uses an ultra-thin plastic coating on a special kind of paper. It can be recharged in just 11 seconds. The battery opens up the possibility of making "smart clothing" that can power things such as mobile phones and music players.

MARIA STRØMME

LIVED: Born 1970

NATIONALITY: Swedish

FAMOUS FOR: Inventing a paper battery that can be charged in 11 seconds

DID YOU KNOW? In addition to doing research on batteries, Dr. Strømme's team is working on a way of releasing medicine slowly into the body over a long period.

LET THERE BE Light!

At the end of the 1800s, electricity was the new source of energy. In the 1880s, power plants began to produce electricity for thousands of homes and factories. The reason was that everyone wanted electric lighting.

This was one of the first light bulbs made by Thomas Edison and his team at his "Inventions Factory" in Menlo Park, New Jersey.

LIGHTING LEADS THE WAY

In the early 1800s, the scientist Humphry Davy produced an arc (a large, bright spark) in a small gap between the two poles of a powerful battery. This was the very first kind of electric light—the arc lamp.

SPARKS AND FIRE

Humphry Davy regularly gave public lectures on science. He was a real showman, and his lectures always drew a crowd. Davy's most important discoveries were new **elements** (chemicals in their simplest form), such as potassium. In his lectures Davy would drop a piece of potassium into water, with spectacular results. The potassium fizzed, steamed, then burst into violent purple flames.

Arc lamps were big and too harsh for ordinary lighting. The first practical light bulbs were invented in 1878 and 1879 by Joseph Swan and Thomas Edison. They contained a thin **filament** (wire), originally made from burned paper. The filament glowed with a bright light when electricity was passed through it.

Incandescent lights (the type Swan and Edison invented) are still widely used today. However, more efficient kinds of lighting have now been developed. These use less energy to produce the same amount of light. Compact fluorescent lights (CFLs) work like the strip lighting used in offices and factories. CFLs use about a fifth the amount of energy of a traditional bulb. But the lights of the future may be light-emitting diodes (**LEDs**), which are light sources in which the electricity flows in only one direction.

Find out more about LEDs on the next pages...

EFFICIENT AND LONG LASTING

LEDs have been used for small lights for many years. <u>Some LEDs are ten times more efficient than ordinary bulbs. They also last fifty times as long.</u> However, until the twenty-first century, LEDs could not produce a good white light suitable for normal lighting.

QUANTUM DOTS

In 2005, a research group at Vanderbilt University was working with tiny pieces of material called "quantum dots." These dots fluoresced (produced their own light) in bright colors when light was shone on them. One researcher, Michael Bowers, made some extremely tiny "dots." When he shone light on them, they produced a warm white glow instead of bright colors.

The Vanderbilt researchers discovered that if they coated a blue LED light with the quantum dots, it produced a soft white light. This was ideal for lighting a room. Several companies are working on developing light bulbs based on this idea. If they are successful, we could soon be using efficient, long-lasting LED lights in our homes.

HEAT AND LIGHT

James Joule (see pages 12–13) first showed in 1840 that heat is produced when electricity flows through a wire. This is what happens in incandescent light bulbs. When electricity flows through the filament, it gets extremely hot (2,500 °C, or 4,500 °F). The heat makes the filament glow brightly.

<u>An incandescent bulb is inefficient *because* it gets so hot.</u> Large amounts of electrical energy are converted to heat instead of light energy. CFLs and LEDs work at lower temperatures, so less energy is lost as heat.

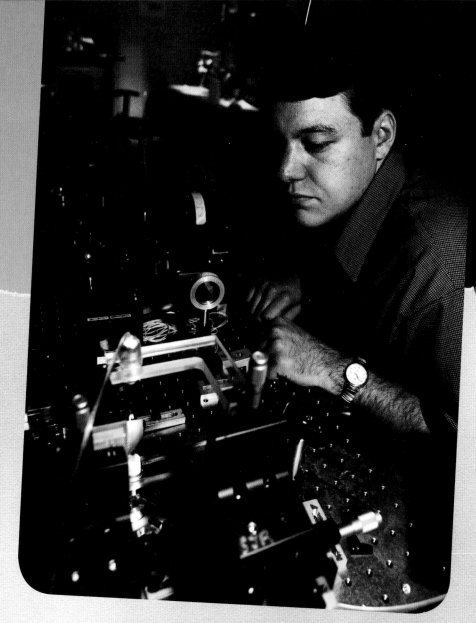

MICHAEL BOWERS

BORN:	1979
NATIONALITY:	American
FAMOUS FOR:	Discovering how to make white LED lights
DID YOU KNOW?	Bowers was part of a research group at Vanderbilt University, led by Professor Sandra Rosenthal. The group studies quantum dots. These could prove useful in lighting, **solar cells**, and display screens.

Oil Takes Over

Electricity is a type of energy that is made using other sources of energy such as heat. Charles Parsons's steam turbine is a very efficient way of turning heat into motion for powering generators. But it needs fuel to work.

In the 1800s, coal powered the world. It was used to heat homes, fuel steam engines and steel furnaces, and power other machinery. Most early electric power plants used coal.

In the early 1900s, large amounts of oil were discovered. Oil was cheaper than coal, it was easier to transport, and it burned more cleanly. Within a short time, oil became the world's most important fuel.

On January 10, 1901, a huge oil "gusher" at Spindletop Hill in Texas blasted tons of drilling equipment high into the air. The oil well discovery at Spindletop marked the beginning of oil as a cheap fuel.

FUEL FROM COAL

In the 1920s and 1930s, the French engineer Eugène Houdry found a way to get more fuel from crude oil. Houdry had trained as an engineer, but in his spare time he drove racing cars. After World War I (1914–1918), he became interested in improving fuels for cars. In the 1920s, there were worries that oil supplies were running out. Houdry began looking for a way to turn lignite (brown coal found widely in France) into useful fuel.

Houdry found a research chemist who had made small amounts of gasoline from coal. The process involved using a catalyst to "crack" (break down) the heavy, solid materials of lignite into lighter, liquid fuels. However, the process was slow and inefficient.

MANY FUELS

Crude oil (petroleum) is a thick, black liquid made up of many different substances. The lighter parts of this mixture can be made into gasoline and other fuels. The heavier parts are heavy oils, waxes, and tars, and are less useful.

EUGÈNE HOUDRY

LIVED: 1892–1962

NATIONALITY: French

FAMOUS FOR: Developing **catalytic cracking**

DID YOU KNOW? Houdry also invented the catalytic converter. This device is used for reducing pollution in modern cars. However, catalytic converters were not widely used until after Houdry's death.

Find out more about catalytic cracking on the next page…

IMPROVING THE PROCESS

Houdry set up a factory to try and improve the process. He tested hundreds of different catalysts. He did manage to make some fuel, but the process was not a commercial success.

In the early 1930s, U.S. oil companies became interested in what Houdry was doing. He moved to the United States and began trying to "crack" the heavy materials in oil. He had much more success. By 1937, the Sun Oil Company was producing fuel using Houdry's catalytic cracking process.

HELPING THE WAR EFFORT

Catalytic cracking was first used widely during World War II (1939–1945). Cracking plants were used to make aircraft fuel from oil waste material. Oil companies were able to get far more fuel from each barrel of crude oil. This was crucial during the war, when oil was in short supply. It helped to keep the Allied forces (the United States, United Kingdom, Australia, and other countries) supplied with fuel.

HIGH-OCTANE FUEL

Fuel for gasoline engines needs to have special properties. Some kinds of fuel burn too easily: they explode in the engine before the spark plug sets them alight. This causes "knocking," which damages the engine. Fuels that knock are called "low octane." High-octane fuels are much better. Catalytic cracking made it possible to produce higher-octane fuels. Better fuels mean that engines run more efficiently.

Petroleum is processed in huge factories called refineries. This modern petroleum refinery is in Singapore.

29

Power from Atoms

During World War II, a new kind of energy was developed. **Atoms** are the very small particles that make up all matter in the universe. At the center of every atom is a tiny, heavy nucleus. The forces that hold the nucleus together are extremely strong. <u>If the nucleus of an atom is split open in the right way, it can release a huge amount of energy</u>. This is nuclear power.

INVESTIGATING ATOMS

The Italian physicist Enrico Fermi built the very first **nuclear reactor** (the energy source in a nuclear power plant). In the 1930s, Fermi was one of a group of scientists who were making new discoveries about how atoms are put together. Fermi found a way of firing neutrons (particles found in the nucleus) at an atom. This changed it into a new element. In 1938, Fermi won a Nobel Prize for this work. Soon afterward, Fermi and his family moved to the United States.

In the same year, scientists in Germany and Sweden discovered that if uranium was bombarded with neutrons, the nucleus split apart and released large amounts of energy. The process was called nuclear **fission**. When Fermi heard the news, he immediately began to set up fission experiments. In 1942, Fermi and the Hungarian scientist Leó Szilárd built a nuclear reactor at Chicago University. It was a huge step on the road to nuclear power.

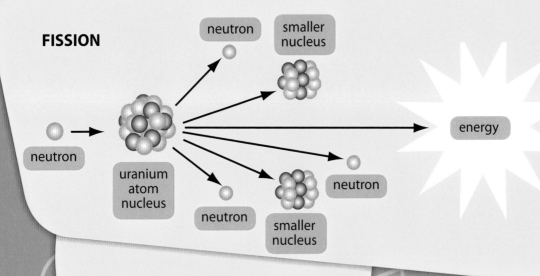

FISSION

neutron

smaller nucleus

energy

neutron

uranium atom nucleus

neutron

neutron

smaller nucleus

Fermi's work was vital in understanding nuclear fission. When a neutron hits a uranium atom, it splits the nucleus into two smaller nuclei and three neutrons. Large amounts of energy are released.

Enrico Fermi is shown here at the controls of the Chicago synchrocyclotron, a device used in his work on atoms.

ENRICO FERMI

LIVED: 1901–1954

NATIONALITY: Italian

FAMOUS FOR: Building the first nuclear reactor

DID YOU KNOW? During the first atom bomb test, Fermi threw some pieces of paper in the air and watched how they were blown by the shock of the bomb. From this "experiment" he was able to quickly estimate (roughly calculate) the power of the bomb. Making a quick estimate like this is often called the Fermi method, in his honor.

NUCLEAR DANGERS

Nuclear power is an important source of energy, but it has its problems. Nuclear fission reactors produce very dangerous radiation (energy waves). An accident at a nuclear power plant could release particles into the air and cause many deaths. The used fuel from a fission reactor also produces radiation. It has to be stored safely for many years to stop it from poisoning the environment.

An accident at Chernobyl power plant in Ukraine in 1986 destroyed buildings, damaged the environment, and caused illness in animals and people.

SAFER ENERGY?

There is another nuclear process that could produce more energy and is safer than fission. Nuclear **fusion** is the process that powers the Sun. The fuel is **hydrogen**. In fusion, hydrogen atoms fuse (join together) to make helium and to release energy.

There are two approaches to fusion research.

1. Fusion reactions are run in a doughnut-shaped container called a **tokamak**. The fuel has to be hotter than the center of the Sun. Magnetic fields (regions where a magnetic force can be felt) stop the fuel from touching the outside of the container and melting it.

2. High-powered lasers are fired at a very tiny pellet of fuel. Some lasers heat up the fuel, while other lasers hold it in place.

So far, fusion research has not produced useful amounts of power. However, large-scale reactors may be the stepping-stones to the first fusion power plants.

INTERNATIONAL SCIENCE

Fusion research involves building extremely large, complex machines. Individual countries cannot afford the huge costs involved. <u>Fusion research is therefore an international effort, involving thousands of scientists, engineers, and managers.</u> ITER is a huge tokamak being built in southern France. The governments of the United States, Europe, Russia, China, Japan, and India are all contributing to the cost.

When it is finished in 2017, the ITER tokamak will be the largest fusion reactor in the world.

Going Back to NATURE

Fossil fuels (oil, coal, and gas) provide most of our energy and electricity. However, they are not ideal energy sources. Supplies of fossil fuels are being used up fast, and new supplies are getting harder to find. Another problem is that burning fossil fuels produces air pollution. This pollution can damage human health. It is also having an effect on the climate (general weather pattern), making the whole world warmer.

Scientists have been looking for better, cleaner sources of energy for many years. The most promising ideas involve harnessing **renewable** sources of energy such as the wind, running water, and the Sun.

One of the first scientists to realize the value of solar (Sun) energy was Maria Telkes. Her work on solar energy earned her the nickname "the Sun Queen."

Maria Telkes (on the left) worked with the architect Eleanor Raymond (right) to design a solar-heated house.

FROM HUNGARY TO THE UNITED STATES

Maria Telkes was born and grew up in Hungary. She first became interested in capturing solar energy when she was still at school. Telkes studied chemistry in college. She moved to the United States in 1925. First she studied the energy of living things. Then she designed a kind of battery that turned heat directly into electricity.

In 1939 Telkes began working at the Massachusetts Institute of Technology (MIT). She turned her "heat battery" into a solar cell that ran on heat from the Sun. (Modern solar cells turn sunlight, rather than the Sun's heat, into electricity.) In 1948 she designed the heating system in a pioneering solar-heated home.

MARIA TELKES

LIVED: 1900–1995

NATIONALITY: Hungarian

FAMOUS FOR: Developing new ways to use solar energy

DID YOU KNOW? Telkes worked on solar heating projects until she was well into her seventies.

This photo shows Maria Telkes in 1963.

CARBON DIOXIDE

When a fuel burns, carbon dioxide gas is one of the main waste products. Scientists have found that the amount of carbon dioxide in the air has been growing for many years. <u>Carbon dioxide is a greenhouse gas</u>. It traps warmth from the Sun and prevents it from escaping into space. The increase in levels of carbon dioxide is one of the main reasons why Earth's climate is slowly getting warmer.

SOLAR HEATING

In 1948 Telkes designed a solar heating system for an experimental house near Boston. At that time practical solar cells had not been invented. Previous solar heating systems had been able to provide only about a quarter of the heat for a house. However, Telkes designed a system that kept the house warm all year, even though winters in Boston are very cold.

Telkes continued to work on solar energy on and off for the rest of her life. She invented a solar cooker and a solar-powered device called a still. The still evaporated salt water and condensed it into fresh water. Small versions of this still were fitted to many lifeboats. In an emergency, the still could produce enough fresh water to keep people in the lifeboat alive.

At this solar power plant in California, curved mirrors focus the Sun's rays to heat oil. The heated oil boils water to drive steam turbine generators.

"I envisage the day when solar heat-collecting shelters ... could develop enough heat from the Sun for pumping into an entire community of homes."

Maria Telkes

OTHER ALTERNATIVES

Solar energy is only one of many "alternative" energy sources. Other kinds of energy are being developed as alternatives to fossil fuels. Hydroelectricity (electricity generated from rivers) is the most developed form of alternative energy. There are also power plants that get their energy from the wind, from the waves or tides, and from underground heat (geothermal power).

Wind power is the fastest-growing type of renewable energy. Wind generators are usually huge propellers. As the propeller turns, it turns a generator. The generator can produce electricity for buildings in the area.

Many wind "farms" are now built off shore. The wind blows more consistently at sea, and the wind turbines can be made much bigger than on land.

FORTH GUARDSMAN

BIOFUELS

Biofuels are another alternative to fossil fuels. They are substances similar to gasoline or diesel fuel that are made from biological material (usually plants). The first kinds of biofuel were made from plants such as corn and sugar cane, which are also food crops. These kinds of biofuel can be almost as bad for the environment as fossil fuels. Tiny **algae** may be a much better way of producing biofuels. The algae can be grown on land that is no good for growing crops, and fed with wastewater (sewage).

SAVING ENERGY

<u>One of the best ways to reduce the dangers from fossil fuels is simply for us to use less energy.</u> Using energy-saving light bulbs (see pages 23–24) and designing cars that use less fuel (see panel on page 39) are two ways to save energy. However, the way to save the most energy is to build energy-saving homes and buildings—just like the house Maria Telkes helped to design in 1948.

Getting energy from the movement of the waves has proved to be difficult. The Pelamis wave power generator is one of several new wave-power ideas being tested off the coast of Scotland in the UK.

USING LESS FUEL

PAC Car II is a demonstration of just how much energy we could save if we tried. It is the most fuel-efficient car ever built. In a competition in 2005, PAC Car II traveled over 20 kilometers (12 miles) on just 1 gram ($^1/_3$ ounce) of fuel. This is equivalent to traveling 12,600 miles per gallon of gas (5,385 kilometers per liter)!

PAC-Car II is not itself a practical car. However, it shows that if we made cars lighter and more efficient, we could make huge energy savings.

FUTURE ENERGY

Scientists around the world are working today on finding energy sources for the future. The focus is on finding energy sources that are renewable and do not produce carbon emissions. Here are just two examples.

POWER FROM SPACE

In 1968 U.S. space scientist Peter Glaser suggested that satellites in space could collect far more solar power than any system based on Earth. His idea for getting the energy back to Earth was to beam it down using microwaves (high-energy waves).

Several groups of researchers have investigated if the idea would work. A study in 1999 by the National Aeronautics and Space Administration (NASA) scientists found that the idea is practical and would have environmental advantages over many other energy plans. The main problem is the high cost of launching satellites into space.

At present space travel is too expensive for Peter Glaser's idea of satellite solar power, but this may change in the future.

FUEL CELLS

Many researchers think fuel cells could be the way to power transportation in the future. A fuel cell is a cross between a battery and an engine. Like a battery, a fuel cell produces electricity. But like an engine, it uses fuel (most often hydrogen gas). The main problem with fuel cells at present is the cost. The most expensive material is platinum, which helps the chemical reaction that makes the fuel cell work. The platinum costs over $2,500 per fuel cell.

A team of scientists at Monash University in Australia have recently found an answer to this problem. The team, led by Professor Maria Forsyth, has developed a type of conducting plastic that can replace the platinum (see below). This breakthrough could make it possible to produce affordable fuel-cell cars in the future.

Professor Maria Forsyth's team at Monash University may have discovered the way to make cheap fuel cells.

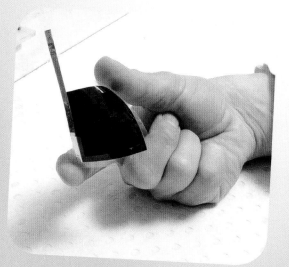

INTO THE FUTURE

Every year there are more people in the world, using more energy. Providing energy that is safe and affordable and does not damage the environment is a huge challenge. However, there is a good chance that scientists and researchers will find new solutions to meet this challenge in the future.

TIMELINE

Follow the colored arrows to see how some of the ideas and discoveries of each scientist influenced other scientists.

Hero of Alexandria
(around 50 CE)

described the very first steam engine. He also invented a wind wheel and temple doors that opened using water power

Alessandro Volta
(1745–1827)

invented the electric battery

Humphry Davy
(1778–1829)

invented the arc light and discovered several chemical elements

Émilie du Châtelet
(1706–1749)

proved Leibniz's theorem that kinetic energy is proportional to the square of velocity (speed)

Thomas Young
(1773–1829)

was the first to use the word *energy* in a scientific sense

James Prescott Joule
(1818–1889)

showed that heat and kinetic energy were both forms of energy, and can be converted into each other

Maria Telkes
(1900–1995)

pioneered the use of solar power

Enrico Fermi
(1901–1954)

built the first nuclear reactor

Michael Bowers
(born 1979) **and Sandra Rosenthal**
(born 1966)

invented quantum dot LEDs

Eugène Houdry
(1892–1962)

developed the catalytic cracking process for improving petroleum fuels

Peter Glaser
(born 1923)

developed the idea of collecting solar energy using space satellites

Maria Forsyth
(born 1970s)

developed a new material that should make fuel cells much cheaper

Charles Parsons
(1854–1931)

developed the first steam turbine engine

Hideki Shirakawa
(born 1936)

discovered plastics that can conduct electricity

Maria Strømme
(born 1970)

invented a paper battery that can be charged in 11 seconds

1 The kinetic energy of an object changes in line with its speed.

2 The body burns oxygen for heat.

3 Energy is never destroyed.

4 Plastic can conduct electricity.

5 Splitting the nucleus of an atom can release a huge amount of energy.

6 Fossil fuels are the ideal source of energy.

Answers:

1 False. Emilie du Châtelet showed that the energy changes in line with the square of its speed.

2 False. The body's energy comes from food. Julius Robert von Meyer was one of the first people to put forward this idea.

3 True. Energy is converted from one form to another, rather than being destroyed altogether.

4 True. Hideki Shirakawa discovered that a plastic called polyacetylene can conduct electricity. Maria Forsyth's team have developed a type of conducting plastic that can replace the expensive platinum in fuel cells.

5 True. Nuclear fission produces huge amounts of energy, but also dangerous radioactive waste.

6 False. Fossil fuels provide most of our energy, but they are running out and they cause pollution.

Glossary

algae living things that make their own food, the way plants do

atom extremely small particle that makes up all matter (substances) in the universe

catalyst substance that speeds up a chemical reaction

catalytic cracking chemical process that uses a catalyst to "crack" (break down) the heavier substances in crude oil into substances that can be used as fuels

efficient works quickly and well with little or no waste

electromagnet magnet that uses electricity to produce its power to attract

element simplest form of a substance, made from only a single type of atom

filament (in a light) thin wire or strand of carbon, often coiled, that glows brightly when electricity is passed through it

fission process of splitting the nucleus of an atom to produce nuclear energy

force push or a pull

fuel any substance that can be burned or processed in some other way to produce energy

fusion process of joining atoms together to produce nuclear energy; process that fuels the Sun

generator machine that produces electricity

hydrogen element that is a very light, colorless, highly flammable gas

incandescent light type of light bulb, with a glowing wire filament inside a glass bulb

joule measurement used to describe a unit of energy

kinetic energy energy of movement

LED short for *light-emitting diode*, a light source in which the electricity flows in only one direction

magnetic field region where a magnetic force can be felt

Nobel Prize international award given each year for physics, chemistry, physiology or medicine, literature, and peace

nuclear reactor strong, closed and shielded container in which nuclear reactions take place

petroleum crude oil; thick, greenish-black liquid found underground that can be processed to produce fuels, oils, plastics, and all kinds of other useful materials

power plant factory that produces electricity from another energy source, for instance, oil, gas, or hydropower

renewable can be renewed, or cannot be used up. Renewable energy sources include solar power, wind power, and biofuel.

solar cell device that converts light from the Sun directly into electricity; also called a photovoltaic cell

square in mathematics, you square a number by multiplying it by itself

tokamak doughnut-shaped container with strong magnetic fields inside it, which is used in some kinds of nuclear fusion research

turbine device like a fan or a propeller that spins when wind or a moving fluid passes through it

Books

Arnold, Nick. *Killer Energy* (Horrible Science). New York: Scholastic, 2009.

Claybourne, Anna. *Forms of Energy* (Sci-Hi). Chicago: Raintree, 2010.

Oxlade, Chris. *Solar Energy* (Fueling the Future). Chicago: Heinemann Library, 2009.

Raum, Elizabeth. *Fossil Fuels and Biofuels* (Fueling the Future). Chicago: Heinemann Library, 2009.

Raum, Elizabeth. *Nuclear Energy* (Fueling the Future). Chicago: Heinemann Library, 2009.

Raum, Elizabeth. *Wind Energy* (Fueling the Future). Chicago: Heinemann Library, 2009.

Solway, Andrew. *Graphing Energy* (Real World Data). Chicago: Raintree, 2009.

Solway, Andrew. *Renewable Energy Sources* (Sci-Hi). Chicago: Raintree, 2010.

Woodford, Chris. *Energy* (See for Yourself). New York: DK Publishing, 2007.

Websites

tonto.eia.doe.gov/kids/energy.cfm?page=pioneers
Find out about more scientists who have helped us to understand energy on this Energy Information Administration (EIA) website.

tonto.eia.doe.gov/kids/energy.cfm?page=timelines
This Energy Information Administration (EIA) website has timelines for different energy sources.

tonto.eia.doe.gov/kids
This is a page of energy games and quizzes on the EIA website.

www.iter.org/default.aspx
This is the website for ITER, a giant tokamak fusion reactor being built in southern France with international cooperation.

lasers.llnl.gov
This is the website for laser fusion research at the Lawrence Livermore Laboratory in California. The power of 192 giant lasers is focused on a piece of fuel the size of an airgun pellet.

www.bbc.co.uk/devon/content/articles/2008/01/30/thomas_ newcomen_feature.shtml
You can see an animation of how Newcomen's steam engine worked on this website.

Places to visit

American Museum of Science and Energy
300 South Tulane Avenue
Oak Ridge, TN 37830
Tel: 865-576-3200
www.amse.org
Explores the history of energy and has hands-on exhibits to explore the science of energy.

Texas Energy Museum
600 Main Street
Beaumont, TX 77701
Tel: 409-833-5100
www.texasenergymuseum.org/default.asp
Learn about the history of petroleum energy and modern technology used in the petroleum industry.

Index